FOR A PICKLEBALL PLAYER WHO HAS IT ALL!

A Fun Book for a Great Pickleball Player

Bruce Miller and Team Golfwell

This is book number twenty-two (22) in our *For People Who Have Everything* gift book series.

Cover by Queen Graphics. All images are from Shutterstock or Creative Commons.

ISBN: 9798866339945 paperback b&w

Around the world, 36 million people play pickleball worldwide. [1]

Getting better. "As you get better, you also need to think that when I talk about a kitchen strategy, you have to think as a chess match. You're trying to move your ball around to create an opportunity to attack.

"And, you need to have a plan in place to create that opportunity. So, moving your opponent around that kitchen is crucial for your improvement, and that's how you become a better player."

-- Advice from Simone Jardim. Brazilian-American professional pickleball player. Simone was ranked the No. 1 woman player in the world from 2016 to 2020.

You have no choice. "You don't play pickleball - pickleball plays you, and it's a funny game name but that goes away when you enjoy playing.

"First, you make a choice to play pickleball, then this choice makes you."

-- **Andy Andrews Scott Fliegelman**, owner of Boulder Pickleball Club and coach, Boulder Colorado.

As long as he can walk. "I never thought I'd say this, as long as I can walk, I'm playing pickleball, I can't wait to get back on the court."

-- **Andre Agassi**, Former World No. 1 Professional Tennis Player and nicknamed *the Punisher*.

Andre Agassi

Chainsaw serve. This service is illegal now according to the 2021 USAP rules. It was known as the "Zane Navratil serve" since he popularized it.

It was done by swiping, brushing or rolling the ball against part of the paddle before tossing the ball in the air when preparing to strike a serve and spinning the ball. Then striking the ball with more topspin to create even more spin.

Even though USAP rules made it illegal in 2021, it's still allowed in unsanctioned games.

You can see a video of Zane demonstrating the chainsaw serve and other ways of spinning the ball while snapping your fingers which he and other players use on YouTube, and the link to it is shown in the reference section of this book. [2]

Quiz Question 1. Joe and Moe are playing against each other in a singles match. Moe is about to serve and he's behind in the score. Moe has excellent hand-eye coordination and decides he's going to dazzle Joe. Moe tosses the ball high in the air, catches it on his paddle, and serves the ball in one continuous motion. Joe says that's a fault.

Is Joe correct?

Answer p. 78.

Pickleball in Central Park. There's a pickleball court in the middle of New York City's Central Park at City Pickle. It's open every day from April through October.

There are 14 pickleball courts there surrounded by shady trees featuring the city's iconic skyline as a backdrop. And you can make reservations. Check out the link in note 2 in the Reference section at the back of this book. [3]

NYC Central Park

A long and healthy life. The Mayo Clinic recently did a research study and found that racket sports increase life expectancy between 6 to 10 years and the reason is a bit unclear since they report they found that racket sports involve more social interaction than individual sports. [4]

According to their study, the varying physical demands of racket sports contribute to their ability to improve cardiovascular health and longevity. Pickleball, tennis, and badminton require balance, coordination, and mental agility which are all good things. Plus, socializing while playing these sports likely enhances the already-known benefits of exercise. [5]

Other studies along these lines were done by the American Medical Association, the Copenhagen City Heart Study, and The British Journal of Sports Medicine, which examined the link between six different types of exercise (racket sports, swimming, aerobics, cycling, running, and soccer) and the risk of early death. [6]

Hit it hard! "You've got to be able to hit the ball hard. Nobody plays golf to putt."

– **Joel Pritchard** (one of pickleball's inventors)

The longest rally. The Guinness World Record for the longest pickleball rally is 16,046 shots! The record was achieved by American identical twin brothers, Angelo A. Rossetti and Ettore Rossetti in Rocky Hill, Connecticut, USA, on 10 October 2021. [7]

The rally lasted 6 hours and 11 minutes!

Angelo and Ettore set this record to bring awareness of children under the age of 5 who die every day of preventable or treatable causes. [8]

The Rossetti brothers.

Inner strength. "Have more than you show, speak less than you know."

-- William Shakespeare

"As we advance in life it becomes more and more difficult, but in fighting the difficulties the inmost strength of the heart is developed."

—*Vincent van Gogh*

What is an "Erne" and how is it done? An Erne is an advanced pickleball shot that was executed and brought to mainstream competitive play by Mr. Erne Perry.

An Erne is a volley that is hit by jumping over or traveling around the non-volley zone (or kitchen), An Erne in pickleball gets a lot of attention since it is done by the player either jumping over the corner of the non-volley zone or running through the zone and establishing both feet outside the sidelines before hitting the volley.

The player must contact the ball on their side of the net, without touching any part of the net or the net post.

As you well know, the USA Pickleball rulebook provides that any contact with the non-volley zone or lines while hitting a volley is a fault. But in doing an Erne you avoid this.

It might be easier to watch this link to visually understand this shot if you're not familiar with it. See the YouTube referenced in the end note for a link to the video showing Erne Perry explaining how to execute the Erne shot. [9]

Be wary and cautious when doing this and do it at your own risk. The most common way to injure yourself in pickleball is falling. You need great timing and balance to do this shot.

Remember to tell your partner you might do an Erne since he or she will need to be ready to cover the middle.

An "Erne" - jumping over the kitchen.

A brief history of the game. In 1965, Joel Pritchard (who later became a US Congressman and the state of Washington's lieutenant governor), with his two friends, Barney McCallum and Bill Bell, invented the game and made the first rules. [10] They used table tennis paddles to hit a plastic perforated ball over a badminton net.

His wife, Joan Pritchard said the name of the game became Pickleball after it reminded her of the pickle boat.

A pickle boat is a name used in rowing or crew sports made up of leftover rowers. Joan said she came up with the name since the sport was created from pieces of leftover equipment from other sports.

Other sources state that the name "pickleball" was derived from the name of the Pritchard family dog, Pickles, but later reports showed they acquired the dog after naming the game.

Some say Bill Bell claimed that he had named the game because he enjoyed hitting the ball in a way that would put his opponent in a pickle.

They later brought the game to Hawaii where it was known as pukaball since "Puka" meant hole in Hawaiian. [11]

Joel Pritchard

It's not boring. "Any boredom goes away after you experience your first forty-ball dink rally."

-- Anon.

It takes over. Funny how a little yellow wiffle ball can completely take over your life.

-- Anon.

Pickleball Puns.

- Pickleball is my life, now – I dill with it.

- Find you a man with fast hands and a soft touch.

- Dinkin' and drinkin' -- the perfect afternoon.

- Get out the mason jars, 'cause I'm a pickling machine!

- Bow down to the pickle queen.

- Usually what's mine is yours -- except the middle balls on my forehand side and those are all mine.

- My opponent was not happy with my serve. He kept returning it.

- "Pickleball can get 'rally' tedious sometimes."

- "Did you hear about the couple that met through pickleball? They're still courting.

The look. The couple that plays pickleball together... is probably going to need therapy. And, behind every man who misses a poach there is a strong possibility of his mixed partner glaring at him.

The look extinguisher -- to avoid further escalation, especially if something is said, it is wise to listen until you are sure the partner feels heard and understood. Understand their feelings and validate those feelings to lessen any impact on your game.

Pickleball motto. "My pickleball motto, however, is Rip, Bang, Win, Cake!

"In other words, Rip the ball, bang the ball, win the match, and celebrate with cake!"

-- **Annaleigh Waters**, Professional Pickleball Player

"For me, joy + play = pickleball. "I'm obsessed and try to play four to five times a week. The court might be the only place in the world where I'm fully in the now."

- **Brené Brown**, Professor & Author, Owner of ATX Pickleballers Major League Pickleball Team.

Quiz Question 2. Joe likes to play a drop serve and before he serves, he has a habit of bouncing the ball and catching it in his hand. After bouncing it several times he drops the ball, and it bounces twice. Then Joe hits a backhand serve with his paddle after the second bounce. Is this a legal serve?

Answer on p. 78.

Lots of courts. Did you know that the JW Marriott Phoenix Desert Ridge Resort & Spa, in Phoenix has 17 professionally surfaced, top-of-the-line pickleball courts?

It also has full-time certified pickleball instructors.

High Court. "Pickleball in The Sky", is reported to be the highest pickleball court in the world. This was reported by Invited, the owner and operator of many clubs. It's located at the Tower Club Dallas and is located on the club's 48th floor, providing 360° views of central Dallas. [12]

The court is reported to be available and rented by non-members and is one of the most unique courts in the world having a 360° view of central Dallas, standing 600 feet above ground level. [13] Food, beverages, and a menu are available and specially made for pickleball enthusiasts.

A bridge between tennis and pickleball. "I absolutely love this sport, I love the game... I kind of want to try to be a bridge in the gap between tennis and pickleball."

-- **Jack Sock**, professional pickleball player and also a winner of four career singles titles and 17 doubles titles on the

ATP Tour, and had a career-high tennis ranking of World No. 8 in singles and World No. 2 in doubles.

Opens "Windows" for everyone. "Everyone from the super young to the super old can take part. It takes minutes to learn the basics, games are short, and all you need is a net, paddle, and ball to get started.

It doesn't take much skill to hit the ball, either, because it doesn't move as fast as a tennis ball. The best thing about pickleball, however, is that it's just super fun."

-- Bill Gates

Unwanted remarks driving a cabbie nuts. A man walks out to the street and catches a taxi just going by. He gets into the taxi, and the cabbie says, "Perfect timing. You're just like Frank."

"Who?"

"Frank Feldman. He's a guy who did everything right all the time," replied the cabbie.

The passenger smirks, "There are always a few clouds over everybody."

"Not Frank Feldman. He was a terrific athlete. He won every pickleball match he ever played. He could dink perfectly -- even if he was blindfolded. He did everything right. An amazing athlete!"

"Sounds like he was really something special."

The cab driver continued, "There's more. He had a memory like a computer. He always remembered the score. He could even help people on the next court remember their score. He remembered everybody's birthday. He knew all about wine, which foods to order. He could fix anything. Not like me. I can't even change a fuse. The last time I tried the whole street blacked out. But Frank Feldman could do everything right every single time."

"Yes, wow! That's a great guy!"

"He always knew the quickest way to go in traffic and avoid traffic jams. Unlike me, I always seem to get stuck in them. But Frank, he never made a mistake, and he really knew how to treat a woman and make her feel good. He wouldn't ever argue if she was in the wrong; and his clothing was always immaculate, shoes highly polished too. No one could ever measure up to Frank Feldman."

"How did you meet him?" asked the passenger.

"I never actually met Frank. He died and I married his widow."

My favorite pickleball game. "My favorite game is the next one."

-- Anon.

Serving strategy. You may already know to make a legal serve in pickleball, you have to hit the ball underhand and from below the waist. If it's a drop serve, you hit it after it bounces once, and in both cases, you serve it so that it lands past the kitchen into the diagonally opposite service court.

There are many strategies. When you are starting out, one strategy is to usually serve deep to get time space, and time to hit a great third shot. Focus on getting a feel for placement instead of power. Precision and control are highly important although it's good to vary your serve to keep your opponent guessing and power is important too.

Roar! "I am woman, see me SCORE!"

-- Anon.

No poaching here! "I'm usually ok with my pickleball doubles partner poaching my shots now and then, but not when we're in a bar!"

-- Anon.

Riddles. Q. How many pickleball players does it take to change a lightbulb?

A. None. Because pickleball players sometimes say, "Out? That's not out!"

Q. Why was the pickleball player frustrated?

A. He was having a mid-court crisis!"

Q. Where does a pickleball player who is half-man, half-horse play?

A. At Centaur Court.

Q. What do a dentist and a pickleball instructor have in common?

A. They both use drills.

Q. Where do pickleball players go for their first formal dance?

A. The PickleBALL.

Q. Why was the pickleball association's website down?

A. They had problems with their server.

Spinning the ball. You may already know these. Topspin, backspin, sidespin, corkspin, etc., and all depend on how you strike the ball, of course.

A **backspin** creates a lift on the ball resulting in a lower and shorter bounce. The ball generally goes downward after hitting it.

Topspin is a forward spin causing the ball to dive or drop faster and usually results in a lower and longer bounce. It tends to make the ball pop upward after hitting it.

Sidespin will make the ball curve through the air and bounce in that direction after hitting the court.

Corkspin or **rifling** is hitting the ball on the side, so it rotates parallel to the ground and perpendicular to the net. It doesn't curve through the air but will bounce to the right or left depending on the side of the ball creating the spin that was hit. There is little downward or upward effect.

Quiz Question No. 3. What professional pickleball player played against Novak Djokovic in tennis when they were youths?

Answer on p. 78.

Funny observations.

"The high-pitched sound of the bouncing ball makes me laugh! Except when I see it going past me."

"The paddles look funny except when someone makes an impressive shot!"

"Judges seem to domineer the pickleball doubles partners – they're too used to controlling the court."

Exercises and tips to improve and maintain your skills.

Serving. Toss the ball in the same spot when you serve to help your consistency and accuracy. Make sure the contact point between the paddle and the ball is below the waist.

Breathing. Establish a routine and breathe between points to keep your head clear and stay relaxed. Breathe in for a count of 5, hold it for a count of 4, and exhale for a count of 6.

Short backswing. Take a short backswing and long follow-through for better consistency and hit deep returns to make the opponent's third shot more difficult.

Set up. Set yourself before contacting the ball and move your weight forward when hitting.

Third shots. Practice the third shot drops with an opponent from different areas of the court. Start on the right side in front of the kitchen line and practice drop shots repeatedly from that same spot. After you successfully make 10 (or any number you decide) drop shots in a row, move back one step and practice until you've made another 10 drop shots, and so on.

Have your practice opponent do the same with both of you moving back until you reach the end of the court. Then start again from the middle of the court and so on until you complete the practice from all areas of the court.

Guide the ball with your shoulder, using as little to no wrist action as possible, and drive with a purpose.

Choose the middle. When in doubt about where to aim a return choose the middle in doubles play as it may confuse the opposing team.

Practice dinking as most coaches say it's the most important shot of the game. Dink with a practice opponent and see who can execute 11 successful attack shots first.

Keep the stoplight system in mind by using the green light, yellow light, and red-light method as follows,

Green light: When a ball pops up above shoulder height, attack and hit down on your shot making sure you get in position.

Yellow light: When a ball bounces higher than the net, attack only if you can get in position.

Red light: When a ball bounces below the net, dink back and don't attack.

Girl power! "She kills me – if we play six games, I'll win maybe two."

> **– George Clooney** on his wife, Amal

Pro Mentality and positive attitude. "Every loss I have ever experienced, I go back to one of my favorite athletic quotes, 'Champions are made by previous experiences.' Meaning every time you lose, you have to critically look at yourself in the mirror and break down why you failed, and learn to get better the next opportunity you get."

     – **Professional Riley Newman** on having a pro mentality.

Blocking shots -- beat the bangers. When you see your opponent ready to attack a shot, some people get an urge to hit it back harder. It's better to deflect it or block it back to reset the point as that is a higher percentage shot.

Keep in mind that the desired result for defensive blocking is absorbing the pace of the ball and resending it to the kitchen area.

If your opponent is about to hit a drive, get into the blocking position with feet slightly wider than your shoulders and raise the paddle in front of your chest keeping it close to your body.

Upon contact with the ball, don't swing but angle the paddle slightly to make sure the ball will deflect above the net. Angle the paddle to the right or left to make it more difficult for the opponent to return the blocked shot.

Simone Jardim has done a YouTube video demonstrating blocking shots with soft hands and check out the YouTube link in the Reference section. [14]

Observations on patience. Leo Tolstoy said, *"Patience is waiting. Not passively waiting. That is laziness. But to keep going when the going is hard and slow -- that is patience. The two most powerful warriors are patience and time."*

Mahatma Gandhi said, *"To lose patience is to lose the battle."*

Napoleon Hill wrote, *"Patience, persistence and perspiration make an unbeatable combination for success."*

Bishop Fulton Sheen said, *"Patience is power. Patience is not an absence of action; rather it is 'timing' that waits on the right time to act, for the right principles and in the right way."*

If you play a lot, you will find it helpful to assume the ball is always going to be returned and having that assumption helps patience.

Catherine Parenteau, who at the time of this writing is ranked No. 3 in the world in Woman's Singles, No. 3 in the world for Women's Doubles, and No. 3 in the world for Women's Mixed Doubles by the Professional Pickleball Association, believes this is paramount, "The main thing in pickleball is to be patient."

Variety. "Every match is completely different based on partners and competitors."

-- **Dekel Bar.** Professional pickleball player. He started playing tennis when he was 9 years old and became a pro tennis player 9 years later. Dekel left tennis due to repeated abdominal injuries and then found pickleball.

Pro views from Ben.

- "Turns out that bending your knees in pickleball is just straight magic."

- "Pickleball: the perfect blend of skill and absurdity."

- "Just a couple of pickleball enthusiasts having a dill of a time."

- "The pickleball court: where a good service can bring a whole new meaning to the phrase 'in a pickle.'"

- "I never thought I'd get hooked on a sport with a name like pickleball, but here we are."

- "I never knew a pickle paddle could be so versatile – it's a weapon, a shield, and a ticket to victory all rolled into one."

- "Who says you can't have fun while getting in a good workout? Not us, pickleballers!"

- "Pickleball: the sport that will leave you with a smile on your face and a sweat on your brow."

-- Ben Johns. Professional pickleball player who, at the time of this writing, is ranked No. 1 in the world for mixed doubles, No. 1 in the world for singles, and No. 1 in the world for Men's Doubles by the Pro Pickleball Association.

Surprise! "My neighbor told me his dog retrieved a pickleball two miles from the nearest courts. Sounds far-fetched."

It's fast. "I just believe that the game in person is so much faster and more athletic than what you see on TV or your computer."

– **Simone Jardim,** professional pickleball player.

Groaners. "I had to use my glasses while playing pickleball. It's a no-contact sport."

"I went to a busy restaurant dressed as a pickleball. I got served right away."

"Never underestimate an older woman with a paddle."

"In pickleball, to err is human; to place the blame on someone else is doubles."

Silly name. ""Despite its silly terms and funny name, pickleball is actually quite a sophisticated game."

-- Bill Gates

Elevated play! There are pickleball courts in Colorado at the Broadmoor's Cloud Camp. It has an elevation of 9,200 feet above sea level and sits high on Cheyenne Mountain.

There are amazing views of Pike's Peak in the distance, but it's only open from May through October. You have to get there by riding a mule, on foot or by SUV.

Why is pickleball so popular and addictive? There are many reasons. Some say the ease of learning how to play the sport makes the game fun and simple. Not a lot of training is needed. The court is smaller than a tennis court. Most anyone can play, including people in wheelchairs.

Some other reasons are it's a good workout as found by a study done by Western Colorado University. They found that players averaged a heart rate of 109 beats per minute and burned 354 calories per hour. [15] That makes it a moderate-intensity workout like hiking or yoga and water aerobics. They also found that players saw improvements in their cholesterol levels, blood pressure, and oxygen uptake, after playing for an hour every other day for six weeks. [16]

It can be played indoors or outdoors. You can play singles or doubles with singles giving you more of an intense workout and been reported that it's good for maintaining hand-eye coordination as well as neuromuscular coordination. [17]

If you've played tennis, ping-pong, squash, or racquetball learning the game and techniques is easier and one gradually learns the strategies and techniques. You usually get better the more you play since you're learning the forces needed for hitting the ball deep, dinking, smashing it, etc.

Others say, it's just simply fun.

Quiz Question 3.5. What do you call a pickleball player who's always sneaky?

Sneaky like a fox

Answer on p. 78

Basic Pickleball shots.

The Third shot. It's a highly important shot above all the rest since the third shot allows you and your partner to move to the kitchen line where the game is really played, and most professionals play a drop shot on the third shot. Drive shots are played a lot less than drop shots on this third shot.

The Service. In tennis the serve is highly important. But in pickleball, the return of service is more important than the serve. Most professionals put speed on the service and send it deep.

The second shot is also sent deep to allow the server to move to the kitchen line. Most professionals say to hit this shot with speed and deep. Shifting your weight forward when serving helps increase speed.

Dinking game. The main goal of professionals is to dink so the ball cannot be attacked. If it's unattackable, it's a successful dink.

Also, study your opponents to see if they have any weaknesses in hitting a forehand or backhand. Use it to your advantage by targeting their weaknesses. Keep in mind some players are better at backhand than forehand. However, if an opponent has a disability, proper etiquette doesn't allow you to take advantage of that disability in recreational play, of course.

Effective dinks take patience and precision. It takes patience to keep dinking and resisting the desire to put it away when that put-away, smash shot isn't available.

Move your opponents around with different dink shot placements including cross court shots since you want to keep your opponent(s) in an awkward position as much as possible, so mistakes occur more often.

Many try to mix in a middle dink intermittently to confuse opponents expecting cross-court shots.

Practicing dinks can be done indoors since you don't need a high ceiling.

Spin shots. Slicing or underspin is usually very effective, especially on the third shot. Topspin is also very effective since the ball tends to drop and doesn't bounce high and is very useful when you have the opportunity to hit a topspin shot to attack. There's also side spin which makes the ball move to the right or left after hitting the ground.

There's a 10-minute video on YouTube demonstrating spin shots. Check out the link in the reference section. [18]

The lob. The lob generally is a low-percentage shot unless it's done at the right time. The best time to lob is after a hitting few dinks back and forth, and you notice your opponent leaning forward.

The Kitchen Line Volley. If your opponent is at the baseline, you have more time to prepare for a return shot. Use a short punching motion keeping the paddle away from your body as that is a higher percentage shot to keep the ball in play.

Get down low when volleying and keep your paddle handle lower than the paddle head to be sure the shot clears the net.

Want to get away and play? This is really getting away. In Northwest Montana, there's not much around except highly spacious and picturesque landscapes with huge and amazing sky views.

There's a pickleball club called the "Two Rivers Pickleball Club." Surprisingly this club has ten world-class pickleball courts, in a remote and unpopulated area.

It's near Flathead Lake about an hour's drive from South Glacier National Park, and has four indoor courts, six outdoor courts, a conference center, and a bar.

Even though it may be remote, players come from all over the world to play pickleball and they do that for an annual tournament event called "The Crown of the Continent" tournament in August. It's named that since that's the nickname for Glacier National Park.

The event has men's, women's, and mixed divisions. Google it if it interests you.

A strategy similar to a chess match. "As you get better, you also need to think that when I talk about a kitchen strategy, you have to think as a chess match. You're trying to move your ball around to create an opportunity to attack."

-- **Simone Jardim**

Pickleball Etiquette.

- Learning Pickleball Official Rules is important since if you are familiar with the rules, you'll be aware of mostly commonsense etiquette principles. *You can download the official rules from the link shown at the end of the Answers to the Quiz questions page on p. 80 of this book.*

- These are common sense and basic etiquette rules, most of which you may already know. Balls frequently stray off from your court as you play and other balls roll into your court. Return the ball - roll it to whoever is waving for it and don't switch balls. It's best to return it as quickly and quietly as you can.

- When your ball strays off your court, call out to the court, where your ball is going letting the players know your ball is on their court to alert them so no one might accidentally roll an ankle. Also, avoid interrupting active play.

- Follow any local rules for lines of paddles waiting to play courts. Ask the regular players what the procedure is to be polite.

- Always be courteous and respectful and use good sportsmanship when playing. Don't deride anyone's ability. Good sportsmanship also means giving people the benefit of the doubt on close-line calls. Play the game with a good attitude and try to make it enjoyable for all. Keep it as a fun game and share the fun with all. Socialize. Pickleball is popular since it's a fun game for all. Tap paddles before and after the game.

- Compliment good shots that the other side made, or your partner made.

- Avoid negative attitudes and negative judgmental opinions.

- Don't walk across courts with players present on them without permission.

- If you're playing badly that day (as every one of us does), keep it to yourself and remember every time you fail it's actually a learning experience to gradually build you to play a better game.

- Basically, use common sense and be respectful to everyone as much as possible so people will have a good time playing.

A mixture of sports. Pickleball is a mixture of tennis, badminton, and ping pong with a side of squash or racquetball.

-- Anon.

Need a "Pickleball Team Name?" Here are a few suggestions,

- Bangers and Smash
- Dink Floyd
- The Ace Bandits
- Dink and Drop
- Take this lob and shove it.
- Pickleball Princesses
- Pickle Power
- Pickled Pink
- The Drop Squad
- The Cuke-est couple
- The Big Pickles
- The Kitchen Sinkers
- The Kitchen Crew
- The Paddle Slammers
- Dinking and Dunking
- The Paddle Kings
- The Big Dills
- The Volley Vultures
- Making a Racket
- The Dinking Divas
- Grippers N' Rippers

- The Dink Sinkers
- Pickleme
- Balls on Fire
- Team Pickle-Up
- The Whippersnappers
- The Pickle Ballers
- The Hot Pickled Peppers
- The backboards
- Dink-a-Lings
- Dill With It
- Balls of Fury
- The Lobstoppers
- Dinking Problems
- Mid-Court Crisis
- The Flapper Jacks
- The Big Dills
- Dill Me In
- The Kitchen Dinks
- The Ballerinas
- Viva las Pickles!
- The Dip Team
- The Cucumbers
- PickleballZ
- The Lobsters
- When Harry net Sally
- Grand Slammers
- The Kitchenettes
- Net Menders
- The Net Results

- The Smart Aces
- The Kitchen Counters
- The Smasheroos
- Baby Got Backhand
- Dink Dynasty
- Party 'til You Cuke
- Volley Llamas
- Dill-ishest Prize Winners
- Rock Lobbers
- The Picklemonsters
- Pickleball Punishers
- The Pickle Pack
- The Pickle Babes
- Paddle Punchers
- Dill-I-Am
- The Slicers
- The Spinners
- Team Smashbomb
- The Picklebombs
- Humble Picklers
- The Addicts
- The Fickle Pickles
- The Smokeballers
- The Best in Brine
- The Fireballers

Strive for consistency. Pickleball is a game of consistency. If you practice hitting dependable shots over and over again, you're going to be a great player wearing down opponents.

Wearing the other side down especially if they are impatient, tends to make them commit unforced errors.

For what their worth here are a few very simple tips,

- Do high-percentage shots. Even though there are a lot of choices on shots to make, focus on the highest percentage shot you know will work. Let's say you're in a rally, and you could either return with a dink or a tougher shot speeding up the ball. Dinks usually have an 80% chance of going in while speeding the ball up shots has a much lower percentage. If you watch professionals, they occasionally and purposely do speed ups or purposely vary speeds when dinking as a strategy if you're an excellent player.

- Patience is power in pickleball. Only attack when the ball rises above your waist.

- You know this and have heard this thousands of times -- that's because it works -- "Keep your eyes on the ball all the way to your paddle and your head still."

- Avoid large backswings and focus on a smooth and controlled swing all the way through.

- You don't have to hit near the sideline. Try going down the middle or two to three feet inside the sidelines and back line.

- Avoid letting the ball get behind you since balls behind you are much harder to hit.

- Anticipate where the ball will be and get to that spot before the ball. Then pause and swing. Shots made when you're running make you look really good but they're actually more difficult when your feet are moving.

- If you're getting higher balls, attack. Opponents will tend to believe you attack anytime and that may get in their head making them think they have to hit a better shot. That results in more thinking on their part, and missing more shots than normal.

The Return of Serve. The team returning the serve has a higher percentage of winning points since they can get to the kitchen line faster assuming the players have equal ability. Missing the return cancels winning that point.

Since most players want to keep that better percentage of winning try to return the serve deep and in the middle. Trying to hit close to a sideline doesn't have as good as a percentage than going deep up the middle.

Quiz Question No. 4. Joe and Moe are playing against each other. These words were exchanged. For what comments can a technical warning be given?

A. "You play like a pro, nice shot!"

B. "Lucky shot you stinkin' bonehead!"

C. "My grandmother plays better than you! She beat your butt last week didn't she, you slow mo!"

D. "Nice smokeball!"

E. Only A and D.

F. Only B and C.

G. All of the above.

Answer on p. 79

Stay with your shot decision. Before hitting a shot have an idea of the shot you want to hit and stay with it. Deciding to change your shot often results in mishits.

Court talk on the lighter side.

"Whose serve?"

"What's the score?"

"Are you 1 or 2?"

"What day is this?"

"Who are you people?"

"Do you know who I am? No, really, does anyone know who I am?"

Hand signals. Hand signals might be used by line judges or players. Here are a few common hand signals.

Hand covering eyes - A line judge's signal that he or she is unable to make a call because their view was obscured.

Pointing the index finger - A call that the ball was out by pointing upward or in the direction the ball went out.

Palm facing down - Indicates the ball was in.

Open palm behind the back - A common signal to the receiver, from the receiver's partner, to switch sides after the return.

Closed fist behind the back - A signal to the receiver, from the receiver's partner, to not switch sides after the return.

Clapping hands - Great winning shot!

The Overhead. When you and your partner are at the kitchen line and the other side hits a lob, think overhead to keep your position. Practicing overheads in this situation is highly beneficial as long as you don't try to smash it. Smashing it causes errors more often than simply trying to keep it in play.

If you played tennis before, get used to the ball dropping slower than a tennis ball since tennis players have a tendency when adjusting to the game to swing early and whiff. This is especially true if you are playing outdoors in windy conditions.

Rip & Bang. "My pickleball motto, however, is Rip, Bang, Win, Cake! Rip the ball, bang the ball, win the match, and celebrate with cake!

-- **Anna Leigh Waters**, Top Professional Pickleball player.

The foot doctor is a good sport. I beat my chiropodist at poker, pool, darts, 5 different video games, and 10 pickleball games in a row. But at no point did he stop smiling. The man knows how to deal with de feet.

The Serve. The serve is the only shot you have 100% control over, and you only get one serve compared to tennis. So, it's important you get your serve in. Take your time when serving.

Hitting the serve deep and with pace makes it more difficult to return and it also results in a longer time for the person who hit the return to get to the kitchen line.

Not getting your first serve in also tends to take a toll on your team's morale for a bit.

Getting the ball in play helps your chances of getting a weak return and gaining the point. You don't go for the sidelines as you do in tennis.

Shift your weight forward to add pace to your serve and generally stay back looking for a deep return -- unless your opponent tends to hit it short more often than not. Even though Joe Pritchard (one of the inventors of pickleball) said, "You've got to hit it hard. Nobody plays golf to putt," consistency gives you a higher percentage of winning a point.

Be in the present. I hope you get to do something that brings you joy this weekend. For me, joy + play = pickleball. I'm obsessed and try to play four to five times a week. The court might be the only place in the world where I'm fully in the now.

-- **Brene Brown**. Author of six No. 1 NY Times bestselling books. She is known for her work on shame, vulnerability, and leadership.

Patience is difficult in all sports. Most pro pickleball players say the lack of patience results in more than not losing the point. That is true in other sports as well. "Having patience is one of the hardest things about being human. We want to do it now, and we don't want to wait. Sometimes we miss out on our blessing when we rush things and do it on our own time."

-- **Deontay Wilder**, Professional heavyweight boxer.

Keeping the shots low over the net. It's not as easy as it sounds. Keeping your paddle parallel to the net versus an open paddle face will tend to keep the shots low over the net.

A low pickleball shot lessens the likelihood of attack shots. Low shots force opponents to hit the ball up increasing your chances for a higher ball that you might be able to put away.

The goal for you and your partner in doubles pickleball is to keep the pickleball low. To do this, consider your paddle angle, as well as the pace you are putting on a pickleball at different heights.

Dinking shots low and crosscourt tend to give you the most margin for error since a cross-court dink usually travels over the lowest (middle) part of the net. A crosscourt dink also gives you more court space to dink into versus a straightforward dink.

Stay patient. If you keep it low, sooner or later your opponent(s) may pop the ball up allowing you to hit an attack shot.

Brings in everyone. It's one of the few sports that brings multi-sports athletes together.

-- **Tyson McGuffin.** Top-ranked professional pickleball player.

Crush and rush. This is also called "Shake and Bake" where instead of the serve returner hitting the usual third shot drop, one player (the shaker) drives it low over the net with pace while the baker "rushes" to the net near the centerline adding pressure for the opposing team to make a poor return. If it's a poor return, the baker puts it away.

Not just for seniors. Tough guys play it -- "We see pickleball as an incredible medium that brings people together, connects communities, and promotes a healthy and active lifestyle."

    -- **Drew Brees**. American former football quarterback who played in the National Football League for 20 seasons

Drew Brees

Avoid injury - the 4 P's of Pickleball. Dr. Sanj Kakar, a prominent hand and wrist surgeon at the Mayo Clinic says people should remember the four "P's" of pickleball to avoid hurting themselves. [19]

The first P is a proper warmup. Stretch and do a warmup before you play. Without a proper warmup, you risk Achilles tendon injuries and other injuries.

The second P is to practice with a purpose. Don't always try to hit the same swing. Vary your motions to avoid repetitive motions that cause chronic overuse injuries.

The third P is proper equipment. Dr. Kakar suggests that as we age squeezing hard on the handle causes stress on the hand and increased pressure on the wrist. Make sure your hand fits well on the grip of the paddle.

The fourth P is proper mechanics. Dr. Kakar says this is the most important P since in his view the motion of hitting is more severe of a motion than the one you make in tennis. Tennis balls bounce higher and pickleball swings are quicker and more violent at times according to the good doctor. [20]

4 P's

Indoor vs. Outdoor. "I prefer playing outdoors more than indoors, even though I spend the majority of my time throughout the year playing indoors. I prefer the outdoors because the ball is a little bit heavier than the one used indoors, and it makes a big difference for me because I get to control the ball much better."

      -- **Catherine Parenteau**, Ranked as high as the 2nd best Woman Professional Pickleball Player in the world.

It's a quick game! Anticipating a shot helps you be a fraction of a second quicker. Don't wait to see where the ball is going after it's hit to you as that may be too late. Look at the angle of the opponent's paddle as he or she strikes the ball so you can start to react and shift your weight in that direction before the ball is hit. Glance or take in with your peripheral vision how his or her feet are positioned for the general direction that the ball will be hit and keep focused on the opponent's paddle and ball.

Watch for spin shots. Most know that moving a paddle high to low is a cut, sideways creates side spin, and low to high is a top spin.

Groaners. What do you call a pickleball player who's always unprepared?

A. A raw pickle

Why did the pickleball players have a bad day?

A. Because they were in a pickle.

Why did the pickleball player cross the road?

A. To get to the other court.

What do you call a pickleball player who's always thinking of himself, cocky and overconfident?

A. A big dill.

What do you call a pickleball player who's always changing their mind?

A. A fickle pickle.

Charges filed. The Feds have just raided the pickleball courts and clubhouse that were used as a front for a large illegal underground crime.

No doubt they'll be charged with racquet-eering.

Not wasting my time. "I had so many people tell me that I was wasting my time with pickleball and that I should be in school instead. I wanted to be successful more than anything in the world."

-- **Kyle Yates**. Professional pickleball player and one of the first professional pickleball players. He's been winning gold medals in pro events for over 10 years after being introduced to the sport as a teenager by his uncle, Mike Welter.

Serve tip. "The key to the serve is hitting the ball with some pace and hitting it deep. One of the things that I try to teach when serving is to make sure all of your weight, all of your momentum, is going forward to increase the pace of the ball."

-- **Dave "The Badger" Weinbach**. Top ranked professional pickleball player.

Pickleball one-liners for players over 65.

- Retirement drives me to dink.

- My retirement plan includes coffee, tacos, and pickleball.

- Never underestimate an old man with a pickleball paddle.

- Pickleball junkie and proud of it.

- World's okayest pickleball player.

- If you wanted a soft serve, you should've gone for ice cream.

- One more pickleball game?

Quiz Question No. 5. Which female professional pickleball player was nicknamed "The Queen of Pickleball", and has dominated the courts since 2019.

A. Anna Bright

B. Anna Leigh Waters

C. Catherine Parenteau

D. Simone Jardim

Answer on p. 79

No matter what sport you play, you can play this. "It's something that levels the playing field, so you might have an NFL player playing with an NBA player, and they're like, 'Hey, we can't compete with each other in our sports, but we certainly can in this sport."

-- **Ben Johns** ranked No. 1 in the world professional men's pickleball singles and doubles.

The first pickleball court. The first permanent court for pickleball was built in 1967 on Bainbridge Island, Washington and it still exists today. The sport, needless to say, has come a long way.

As of February 2023, there are over 10,000 courts in the US. In comparison, there are between 15,000 and 16,000 golf courses in the US and golf has been around a lot longer.

And it's about equal between men and women players with 53% of players being male and 47% being female.

A second chance. "The thing about pickleball is that you get a second chance. So, you still can come back and win gold even if you lost."

-- Simone Jardim

A pro's view on being aggressive. "I also believe that I play my best when I hit aggressive shots, so I try to play as aggressively as possible during matches."

-- **Anna Leigh Waters**, Top Professional Pickleball player.

Quiz Question No. 6. After winning a choice of end, serve, receive, or defer, Joe's team chooses to serve. Before the match begins, Moe, Joe's partner, tells the referee that Joe isn't himself today and Joe forgot they previously agreed to receive. Can the Joe & Moe team change their mind and decide to receive?

A. Only the 2nd team to choose may change their choice.

B. Yes.

C. They cannot change their choice once made.

Answer on p. 79

The largest Pickleball Tournament. The largest pickleball tournament in the world is the Minto US Open Pickleball

Championships. Held in 2023, in beautiful Naples, Florida, it attracted over 3,000 players competing.

Pickleball Magazine described the Minto US OPEN Pickleball Championships as the "Tourney for the People".

Players came from all US states and 29 countries from around the world. Ages ranged from 8 to 88.

It's a seven-day event and keeps growing every year!

Quiz Question No. 7. Tiny Tia is a petite woman and wants more power, so she adds lead tape to her paddle to add weight. Is she allowed to do this?

A. Yes, she can do that.

B. No, that's not allowed.

Answer on p. 79

An alternative third shot. Zane Navratil is a high-ranking professional player who suggests there is a third alternative to the two normal choices of either dropping the third shot into the kitchen or driving the third shot.

Zane suggests a hybrid semi-soft drive that he describes as a "hybrid drop/drive shot" that your opponent has to return at an upward angle to you.

He explains it's done by taking the pace off a bit of a drive shot so that it comes in low to your opponent's feet. [21]

Zane Navratil

CPA training helped Zane. My ability to remove my ego to see objectively what is going on in a match. My CPA training gives me an opportunity to look at the game in an accountability way, by the numbers, percentage pickleball. There is risk, reward, and return on investment.

-- **Zane Navratil.** Zane won three state tennis championships, then played tennis in college for Wisconsin-Whitewater. He was a Certified Public Accountant for about a year then decided to become a professional at pickleball.

If you played tennis remember these. If you played tennis, you may know a tennis court is 78 feet long. The pickleball court is only 44 feet long. So, you don't need a long stroke to hit it deep.

Some say "When it's shoulder high, let it fly" when adjusting from tennis to pickleball but it's hard to tell if you're new to the game. Seasoned players as they learn and master the game become gradually adjusted to the court's size.

A shorter court also makes a lob shot more difficult. Keep in mind a lob is a great surprise shot if all players are at the kitchen line and one of your opponents is leaning forward.

The ball doesn't travel as fast as a tennis ball. It's like a whiffle ball and doesn't bounce as high as well, of course. If you're new to the game, try a shorter backswing as returns come back quickly so be ready for it.

Watch out for the sidelines since the court is narrower and tennis angle shots may go wide. Players always seem to adjust to the size of the court.

Underspin is a greater weapon in pickleball than it is in tennis. It is much more effective in pickleball than in tennis especially if everyone is at the kitchen line using dinks.

Underspin has a good chance of making your opponent hit it into the net. Underspin is also effective if you're able to follow up with a top spin shot to keep your opponent guessing.

Be ready. To make sure you are in position, tell yourself you expect every shot your opponent makes is going to be within the lines.

If you've played for a while, you already understand almost nothing surprises you, especially if you're playing outdoors. A deep shot may look like it's going out, but the wind has its way with the ball. So, get ready. If it goes out, it's out and you win the point. If it stays in, you'll be ready to return it.

I'm ready! You probably know this already. In tennis, you normally hold the racket at the 12 o'clock position so you're ready to hit either a forehand or backhand volley.

In pickleball hold the racket in the 11 o'clock position slightly favoring the backhand if you are righthanded. If the ball comes straight at you at a high speed, it's easier to quickly backhand it back, yet you are still able to switch to forehand if needed.

Helpful suggestions. You probably know most of these but there may be new tips or ideas in these suggestions to help you play more effectively or give you a refresher to improve your game.

- If only one of the other team players is at the kitchen line and the other is back, hit it short or at the feet of the player who is back. Or if it's an attackable shot, hit it at the feet of the player closest to the net since he or she has less time to respond to it than the player who is further back.

- During warm-up, see if your opponent is weak at the forehand or backhand and test it out. Hit right at the player to see which side the player favors.

- Hit lobs diagonally as the cross-court is a bit longer. Direct shots from one baseline to the other baseline is 44 feet and diagonally it's about 48 feet. Top spin lobs are the most effective.

- Practice and improve the third shot. Most of the time you face opponents who are already at the kitchen line. It's been said most of the professionals hit a drop shot 75% of the time and a low driving shot or hybrid drop/drive shot the other 25%.

- Notice spins. Practice hitting spins back and make necessary adjustments to your return. Answer under spins with top spins, shots hit with paddles swinging left to right will tend to make your shot go to the right and vice versa.

- When every player is at the kitchen line, if a ball isn't about your knees don't try to hit an aggressive shot. There is a high percentage of errors if you try to put it away. Hit low shots may go long. It's better to be patient and wait for a shot you can attack. In other words, when the ball is low - don't go!

- When you return a serve try to hit it to the backhand side if the player has a weak backhand.

- Above all, keep in mind it's best to just keep putting the ball back in play.

- Drop shots can be more effective if you hit the shot to the middle of the kitchen more toward one of the player's backhand.

- Mix your serves. Vary placement, speed, and spin so you're not predictable by your opponent. Vary your position at the baseline when serving and hit to different areas. Remember to stay back on your serve because of the two-bounce rule.

- Wear out the weaker player. Tell your partner Get with your partner to hit shots at the weaker player. You have a better chance of winning and the weaker player will be motivated to practice more. For example, if one of your opponents has trouble hitting volleys, overheads, backhands, etc, your team should take advantage of it.

- Call out shots to your partner like "mine", "yours" "that's out", etc., during play. Decide whether middle shots should first be taken by the forehand player before you begin play. If you are a right-hander and your partner is a left-hander discuss it thoroughly and clearly.

- If the opponents are holding their paddles at the 11 o'clock position favoring the backhand, hit hard low shots to their forehand. Many players favor hitting backhand volleys and a hit to their forehand side may surprise them.

- No need to try to hit the ball just clear of the top of the net. Chances are trying to be too precise will cause the ball to go into the net. Try higher and softer shots to drop into the kitchen and your percentage of winning the shot will increase.

- When in doubt where to return the ball the middle of the court is a good choice since it may confuse the other side or who will play it.

- If you are going to hit a lob, try to hit it over the player to his backhand side.

- The general rule for returning the serve is simply to hit it back and keep it in play. It's frustrating and a bit demoralizing not to make a return. Generally, have a plan and decide before the serve where you are going to forehand or backhand return it to. Don't be afraid to return it with pace directly at the middle of the player's body or right or left shoulder. The whiffle ball doesn't hurt like a tennis ball does.

- Loosen the grip when dinking. If you hold the paddle too tight it will pop up the ball further than a loose gripped shot. On a scale of 1 - 10 try holding it 4 to 5, or even 3 to 4.

- When playing doubles, move with your partner as a team. Position yourself to cut down the angle that your opponent has to return from. If one of you moves to the far right or left, move to cover the middle.

- Play faster when you are on a roll with points. Keep the winning momentum going.

- If you a playing with a weaker player, slow down the play and take it as an opportunity to try practicing drop shots, lobs, new serves, etc.

- Attack shots. When you have the opportunity to attack, aim at the opponent's feet or to an open area.

- Don't be afraid to poach. If there is an opportunity to cross over to the other side of the court, take it as it usually catches your opponent off guard. Let your partner know you poach occasionally so your partner can cross over too and not leave a side of the court open.

It all comes together. "Pickleball. It's where friendship, laughter, and ridiculous paddles come together."

-- Anon.

The Golden Pickle. A "Golden Pickle" is a term or slang name for a game where one team wins the serve and continues serving the whole game not allowing the opponents to serve or score a point.

It's fast! "I just believe that the game in person is much faster and so much more athletic than what you see on TV or on your computer."

-- Simone Jardim

Quiz Question No. 8. Moe is serving, and in the middle of his service, he's calling out the score especially for his partner Joe who suffers from forgetfulness. Is it a fault if Moe contacts the ball while he's calling out the score?

A. No.

B. Yes.

Answer on p. 80

Shot excuses. We all know we learn from mistakes. Learning the reasons why a shot went bad helps you improve. Excuses are used to deflect potential blame for bad shots and can become a habit. Funny excuses help us to get out of that bad habit. They lighten the situation and help you to relax and play better.

Joe: "The sun was in my eyes. I forgot my sunglasses."

Moe: "We're playing indoors, Joe…"

Joe: "Oh, it's that light - it's way too bright!"

A few more,

- "I would have made that shot if I were 40! But that's been over 30 years from now."

- " I didn't see it, but it looked like it was out."

- "The ball is too hard."

- "My partner is a ball hog."

- "The court is too fast."

- "The court is too slow."

- "The net is too tight."

- "Those playing next to us keep hitting their ball in our court."

- "I can't talk and play at the same time."

- "I need a new paddle. This one doesn't work."

- "I'm hungry. When's lunch?"

- "My partner blocked my view."

- "I thought my partner called that."

- "My partner can't play."

- "My partner is too slow."

- "My partner doesn't know how to serve."

- "My partner doesn't know the rules of the game."

- "Where did my partner go?"

- "The ball took a strange bounce."

- "I was trying not to hit you."

- "It's always the wind."

- "What's the score? Whose serving? 1 or 2? What day is this? Where am I? Why are they looking at us like that? Who are these people?"

Placement versus power. Most agree that pickleball is more about placement than power. By keeping the ball in play in doubles, the team that makes fewer unforced errors usually wins. According to USA Pickleball, 75 percent of rallies are won (or lost) because of errors; only 25 percent are actually earned or won by a good shot. [22]

It's difficult to hit a winner every shot, so placement results in your waiting for the other team to make a fault. The safest place to hit is in the middle to avoid going out of bounds and shots in the middle tend to cause confusion.

Placing the ball at your opponent's weaknesses such as the backhand is good especially when serving. Most players have a weaker backhand than their forehand but that may not be true with everyone, of course, as others have stronger backhands.

End of the session. Many just simply have a great deal of fun playing and watching others play and are sad to see a session end. Stay positive and remember Dr. Suess once wrote, "Don't cry because it's over. Smile because it happened!"

Lobs. Most points are scored when both partners are at the kitchen line. If you find you and your partner struggling to get into the Non-Volley Zone Line, you might want to hit a lob to give you more time such as a lob return of serve.

If you are playing outdoors, be aware of the wind and the chance of high shots blown away out of bounds.

If you have a banger opponent, lobs result in a higher bounce that makes it easier for the banger to drive the ball back, of course.

If everyone is playing at the kitchen line and you see your opponent(s) leaning forward hit a lob over the opponent who is leaning forward.

Anticipate lobs. If your partner is at the kitchen line, be wary of a lob over his head and call your partner off the shot and cover it.

When returning a lob get back to get under it or slightly behind it, keep your feet moving quickly, and step forward with a full swing to hit it. It's difficult to return a lob when moving backward.

It's best to hit a lob in the air. Waiting for it to bounce gives your opponent time to advance to the kitchen line. But when you lose it in the sun or lights, or if you don't have time to get under it, run around it. Don't backpedal to hit a lob and turn and run around it if you have to.

The name of the game. "It is what it is. Once you're into it, you don't even think about the name anymore."

-- **Ben Johns** ranked No. 1 in the world professional men's pickleball singles and doubles.

Move your opponent. So, when you get to the kitchen line, you need to have a plan in place to create that opportunity. So, moving your opponent around that kitchen is crucial for your improvement, and that's how you become a better player.

-- **Simone Jardim**

"Underhand serve" The term "underhand serve" is not used in the Official Pickleball Rules. Instead, the rules specify that a volley serve is made while the player's hand and paddle are moving forward with an upward arc. Oddly, the rules do not appear to state yet that a drop serve must also be made in this way. That is probably so since dropping a ball before serving it has to be hit while the player's hand and paddle are moving forward in an upward arc.

When you're there to win. "As soon as you discover which opponent has less skill with the third shot, send all return-of-serve shots to this person."

— **Joe Baker**, excerpt from "At the Line Pickleball: The Winning Doubles Pickleball Strategy."

Quiz Question No. 9. Joe and Moe are about to begin a match against Helen and Ellen. Joe and Moe have played them many times before but haven't ever won a game against the ladies.

Joe tries to build his own confidence and tells the ladies they aren't going to get a single point against them this time as Joe is going to serve out the whole match by serving 11 points in a row. Helen tells Joe the ladies might get a point even though the ladies don't win a rally as a serving team.

Joe says, "You don't know the rules, you not so bright person. Don't you know only the serving team gets a point when they win a rally." Is Joe correct?

A. True

B. False

Answer on p. 80

How it began for a champ. "We started playing pickleball every day for two weeks. Me and my mom just fell in love with it."

-- **Anna Leigh Waters**, Top Professional Pickleball player.

One serve. Unlike tennis, you don't get a second chance when serving. Most pros say serve deep and to opponent's weakness which is often their backhand.

Hitting the serve deep pushes the opponent back making it a bit more difficult for the opponent to hit a long return. If it's a shorter return, then it's an easier third shot for you or your partner.

Bright future. "I don't think it's caught on nearly enough yet in other parts of the world… but I think anywhere it does start is going to see a similar trend in the US, which is just rapid growth, and once that happens in other areas, I think it would be perfectly suited to the Olympics. It's just you can't rush growth."

-- **Ben Johns** ranked No. 1 in the world professional men's pickleball singles and doubles.

Quiz Question No. 10. From August 2021 to August 2022, approximately how many people played pickleball?

A. 2,000,000

B. 36,500,000

C. 79,500,000

D. 980,000

Answer on p. 80

It's diverse. "On the same court, you can have a millionaire with someone living paycheck to paycheck. No one's interested in what you do for a living, only in how long you've been playing."

-- **Simone Jardim**, Professional Pickleball Player.

How would you describe pickleball? The popularity of the sport and playing often can change your body and help you become an active athlete. So how do you tell others about this sport? Here are some descriptions from professional players.

- It's like tennis, ping pong, and badminton, with a side of racquetball thrown in.

- The perfect sport to get your heart rate up. It's easy, the rules aren't hard to follow, and you make new friends, all rolled up in one!

- Impressive shots with a strange and unique paddle.

- It's getting off your butt and exercising, but it's not flat-out high-intensity exercising.

- The perfect blend of skill and absurdity.

- Pickleball is a great game for players of all ages and abilities leading to miraculous shots or crazy mishaps.

- The lower net creates amazing shots you haven't ever seen before or thought of. That's fun.

- "Too many people don't know what (pickleball) is, and I have to explain it, and it's a lot of effort. It is what it is; once you're into it, you don't even think about the name anymore."

Unwanted nickname. "They call me the 'Seth Curry of pickleball'. All of my shots are nothing but net."

-- Anon.

More reasons for the popularity. There are many reasons. A few are exercising the body and mind, maintaining and perhaps enhancing agility, balance, reflexes, and hand-eye coordination, without overly straining your body.

There certainly seem to be a lot of benefits besides helping to maintain yourself as you age. It is a sport open to all ages and popular with both genders of any age.

A game for everyone. "I can see how people think it's an old person's sport before I started playing, I thought the same thing. Then my mind was blown."

-- **Anna Leigh Waters** (15-year-old pickleball sensation)

More strategies.

- Serve from near the centerline so you can get at most returns more easily.

- If you have the opportunity, hit deep forcing shots into the corners, so your opponent doesn't have time to set up and you get a better chance to come up to the kitchen line. Then hit a passing shot.

- Any shot often used makes you more predictable.

- Face your opponent when returning a service so you have a better position to return a shot to either side.

- If you're playing singles against a good player, don't hit a drop shot when your opponent is deep since they get to it quickly and get in a good position to play a passing shot.

- Vary your shots as this makes you more unpredictable to your opponents.

- In singles, stay closer to the center line but move left or right a bit as your opponent moves.

- In singles, if your opponent is at the non-volley line and you're still back, generally there are three options, 1) A hard passing shot; 2) A drop shot that hits the ground at your opponent's feet; 3) A lob. But keep in mind a lob is a difficult shot when you want to hit it deep enough so that a good player doesn't put it away.
- In doubles, one strategy the Johns brothers used when they played against Matt Wright and Riley Newman in

the 2022 PPA tournament of champions in a four-game match, was choosing who to return the ball to for the third shot. The Johns brothers returned 94 serves to Riley Newman and returned only 2 serves to Matt Wright. They did this because Riley is a great poacher and they successfully kept him back to hit the third shot.

More physical health benefits of Pickleball. Doctors report that the sport not only gives all the benefits of regular exercise, but there are also other benefits. [23]

Pickleball provides all the benefits of regular exercise plus some extra perks.

- Lower blood pressure
- Stronger muscles
- Improved flexibility
- Better balance and agility
- Possible weight loss
- Better footwork
- Improved eye-hand coordination [24]

Most any exercise helps cardiovascular health and that's good for the brain. Also, keeping the current score engages a player to use short-term memory, plus knowing the rules, strategies, etc. [25]

Pickleball and Mental Health. A recent extensive medical study by Frontiers in Psychology was reported by the National Center for Biotechnology Information in February 2023.[26] The study concluded "The results show significant improvements in the different psychological variables measured in pickleball practitioners: personal wellbeing, life satisfaction, depression, stress, happiness, etc."

It was clearly shown that the benefits of the sport of pickleball shows potential as a new tool to work and improve people's mental health. [27]

Pickleball party activities. If you are planning a pickleball party for your group, you might want to include these activities for more fun.

- Pickleball juggling contest. See who can juggle the longest or who can juggle the most balls at once.

- Have a rectangular cake colored like a pickleball court and a miniature net.

- Playing helps your balancing abilities. Try a game on who can balance a pickleball on the head for the longest time. Add distractions to make it even more fun.

- Pickleball trivia games. See who knows the most about the game. Use the facts in this book for trivia games.

Divide up into teams to see which team knows the most. Pickleball rule questions are useful too.

- If you're having a party by a court, hold a mini tournament with prizes such as a big jar of pickles, a bottle of wine, a hilarious trophy, or whatever you come up with. Having a tournament will get your guests to mix even more and get to know each other. Use a round-robin format for your tournament and make up teams by pairing new players (or players with less ability) with more experienced players (or exceptional players).

In a single round-robin tournament, each team plays one game against another team until all teams have competed against each other. The championship team is the team with the most game wins. If there are only a few teams, have a double-round robin tournament, where each team plays against another team twice and the team with the most victories are the championship team. If there is a tie, have a one-game playoff adding a bit of drama and more fun to the party!

Have a piccalilli grand prize such as a funny, hilarious trophy, cucumbers, or whatever you decide.

- Musical Courts. If there are several courts available, play musical courts and have the players march to the music around the courts and play at the nearest court when the music stops.

- Another version of musical courts, which is a good mixer, would be to have everyone play while the music is playing. When the music stops, they stop playing and find a new partner on a new court or something along those lines.

The future of pickleball. Tom Brady, six-time Grand Slam Champion, Kim Clijsters, and other high-worth celebrities and sportspersons are investing in purchasing part interests in major league pickleball expansion.

Other high-worth, smart investors such as Gary Vaynerchuk and hedge fund manager Marc Lasry have also invested in Major League Pickleball expansion.

As you well know, top celebrities including Leonardo DiCaprio, Melinda Gates, the Kardashians, Stephen Colbert, and many others have become involved in playing pickleball.

According to a Harvard Economic Review, "Pickleball shows significant untapped potential from an economic perspective…" [28] The growth of the sport and the increase in people viewing generally means more sponsors, advertising, television rights, ticket sales, and consequently will increase the prize money in tournaments attracting more professional players throughout the world.

Most feel pickleball shows much potential to grow attracting even more investors, celebrities, and wider audiences, all encouraging more to play the sport. [29]

So, the future looks rosy for the sport which almost anyone can play with its simple rules and ease of learning. Above all, have fun, enjoy yourself and encourage others to join in this wonderful sport!

International. The IFP was established in 2010 by the USA Pickleball Association to serve as the World Governing Body of pickleball. [30] It has around 70 member nations.

It holds an annual event, The Bainbridge Cup, named after the island, where the game was invented.

The tournament consists of age and skill divisions for men's, women's, and mixed doubles. It also has a men's and women's singles division that was established recently in 2021.

Above all, have fun! Who says you can't have fun while getting a good workout? Pickleball is a sport that leaves you smiling with a good overall feeling and many other benefits to maintain a healthy life and good disposition!

Answers to Quiz Questions.

1. True. Catching the ball on your paddle when in the process of serving (or during a rally too) is a fault.

2. It's a legal serve. Rule 4.A.8 of the USA Official Rulebook (2023) provides, "The Drop Serve. The drop serve is made by striking the ball after it bounces on the playing surface and can be made with either a forehand or backhand motion. There is no restriction how many times the ball can bounce nor where the ball can bounce on the playing surface."

3. Joey Farias was one of the top 10 youth tennis players in the world from ages 13-18 and frequently played against Novak Djokovic.

3.5. The question was, "What do you call a pickleball player who's sneaky?"

Answer: A sly pickle, or if it's a sneaky serve, then call it a "Nasty Nelson". A Nasty Nelson is when the serving player deliberately attempts to hit the non-receiving player's opponent on the serve. If a serve hits either player before it bounces, the ball is dead, and it is considered a fault by the player who was hit.

4. Answer is F. Only B & C. 13.G.1.a. states that any objectionable language directed at another person can warrant a verbal or technical warning. 13.G.1.b. states that profanity used for any reason can also warrant a verbal or technical warning.

5. B. Anna Leigh Waters was dubbed "The Queen of Pickleball" in a 2019 Washington Post article and the name is apropos as she has been dominating and ranked No. 1 in the world and is she's only a teenager.

6. D. They cannot change their choice once made. Rule 5.A.1. specifically states that once a selection has been made, it cannot be changed.

7. A. Yes. She can do that. Rule 2.E.5.a. includes lead tape as one of the alterations that are allowed. The rule provides, "2.E.5. Alterations. The only alterations or additions that can be made to a commercially made paddle are edge guard tape, lead tape, changes to the grip size or grip wrap, and adding name decals and/or other identification markings on the paddle face. Decals, markings, and tape can extend no farther than 1.0 inches (2.54 cm) above the top of the grip nor more than 0.5 inches (1.27 cm) inside from the outer edge of a paddle or paddle edge guard if in place. Altered paddles must meet all specifications."

8. B. Yes. Rule 4.M.11. calls for a fault if the server "hits the ball to make the serve while the score is being called."

9. B. No. Joe's wrong. Rule 4.F. explains another way a team can be awarded a point - when a technical foul is called against the opponent, but the opponent's score is zero. Instead of taking a point from the opponent, the serving team is awarded a point.

10. B. 36,500,000. This is according to a news report by the Association of Pickleball Professionals released exclusively to CNBC. [31]

Free Official Pickleball Rulebook. Do you want to know more about the rules? At the time of this writing, there is a free download of the USA Official Pickleball Rulebook at this link > https://usapickleball.org/docs/USA-Pickleball-Official-Rulebook-v8-14-2023.pdf

A Brief Glossary. Some of these terms you may know, and some may be new to you.

APP - The Association of Pickleball Professionals.

ATP (Around the post) - A legal shot that travels around the net posts, allowing its trajectory to stay below the height of the net. [32]

Bagel - A shutout. One team earned no points in a standard game ending in 11-0.

Zero Mostel

Baker. The baker is one of the players in a doubles strategy known as "Shake and Bake". Instead of the usual third shot drop, one player (the shaker) drives it low over the net with pace while the baker rushes to the net near the centerline adding pressure for the opposing team to make a poor return. If it's a poor return, the baker puts it away.

Banger - A guy or gal who hits mostly powerful drive shots.

Bash - A hard shot that hits the top of the net and lands in play on the opponent's side of the court, often changing direction and speed.

Bert - In doubles, a poach shot where a player crosses in front of their partner to execute an Erne on their partner's side of the court.

Body shot - A shot made that hits your opponent's body and wins the point. Take care not to ever aim at the head, neck, or other sensitive spots.

Bounce it! - Called out in doubles by your partner asking you to allow it to bounce first before hitting it back as it may land out of bounds.

Chicken wing. This is a defensive shot with a paddle arm and the elbow is bent and extended upwards away from the body. It's used to defend a shot made to the shoulder on the paddle side of the body.

Chop, Chip, Cut, or Slice shot. Striking the ball with your paddle open-faced and moving your paddle downward.

Closed face. Tilting the paddle face down when striking the ball with the upper edge of the racket angled forward.

Continental grip. The most popular grip used. Holding the paddle handle so your first finger and thumb form a "V" directly lined up with the edge of the paddle.

Dead ball. Play stops when a service fault, ball strikes a permanent object, or a hindrance is called.

Dink. A soft shot to the opponent's kitchen.

Dinker. A Player that's good at dinking.

Double hit. Okay as long as the double hit occurred in one continuous stroke.

Drive shot. A powerful groundstroke or volley hit fast and low over the net to the opponent's backcourt.

Drop shot. A soft return shot made from the backcourt or mid-court, after it bounces, that lands in or near the opponent's kitchen.

Drop volley. A soft return shot made from the backcourt or mid-court striking it before the ball bounces and lands in or near the opponent's kitchen.

Erne. A volley hit near the net by a player outside the court or jumping outside the court. Named for Erne Perry, the first one who used the shot in mainstream competitive play.

Fault. An infringement of the rules that ends a rally and results in a dead ball.

Foot fault. Failure to keep both feet behind the baseline when serving when the paddle hits the ball. Or, when volleying stepping on or into the non-volley zone or if your momentum carries you there when volleying.

Groundstroke. Striking the ball after it bounces.

Half Volley. A groundstroke struck low to the ground immediately after the ball bounced.

Hinder or Hindrance. An interference of play by something outside of the game. For example, another ball rolling across the court or a person or animal crossing the court. If called, it's a dead ball and the point replayed The dead ball occurs as soon as a hinder is called by either side. Exception: if it's determined it was an invalid call, the point is not replayed and the side calling the hinder loses that point.

IFP. The International Federation of Pickleball is a federation of national pickleball organizations. The International Federation of Pickleball was created to act as the world governing body for the sport of pickleball. The IFP was founded in 2010 by the USA Pickleball Association, now USA Pickleball. [33]

A Joey. Remember the "Around the Post" (ATP) post shot? It is a legal shot that travels around the net posts, allowing its trajectory to stay below the height of the net. A "Joey" is hitting the ATP shot directly back at the opponent that made the ATP shot. Named for Joe Valenti. There is a YouTube video referenced in the references showing a "Joey" in slow motion. [34]

Let serve. When a served ball hits the net and lands in the correct service court is considered a valid serve under USAP rules.

Lob shot. Hitting it high over the opponent's head and landing in the opponent's backcourt.

Misdirection shot. This shot is when a player intentionally wants to deceive the opponent and prepares to hit the ball in a certain direction but at the last instant hits the ball in an unexpected direction or pace.

The Nasty Nelson. A serve that intentionally hits the non-receiving opposing player closest to the net, rewarding the point to the server. [35] Named for Timothy Nelson. Check out the shot on YouTube referenced in the references section. [36]

Non-volley zone, NVZ, or "Kitchen". It measures 7 feet (2.1 m) by 20 feet (6.1 m) and includes all lines. It's an area adjacent to the net and volleying from the kitchen is not allowed. If a player's momentum carries the player into this area after volleying the ball, it's a dead ball and that player incurs a fault. Not sure, but it's been reported that the non-volley zone got its name from the game of shuffleboard that also has a kitchen area which has a 10-point penalty.

Open-faced shot. When you tilt the paddle face up when striking the ball.

Out. A line call made when a ball lands outside the court lines. Or if it's a serve, the ball lands outside the service court. Can be indicated by pointing up or in the direction of the out ball.

A call is made by a player after the ball hits the ground, and if so, it's considered to be a line call and a deadball results.

But if the ball is determined to be inside the line, it's a fault for the team making the call.

If the player calls "out!" before the ball has hit the ground, then it's considered communication between the players telling a player not to hit it.

Pace. That, of course, is the speed of the ball. Players purposely vary the tempo and speed for advantage over the opposing team since the other team doesn't know what to expect.

Pantry. Refers to the area outside the court on either side of the kitchen. If a player does an "Erne" shot, he or she jumps over the kitchen and lands in the pantry. When a player jumps over the kitchen to execute an Erne shot, the player lands in the pantry.

Permanent object. Anything near or above the court such as the ceiling, etc. and if a ball hasn't bounced and hits a permanent object, it's a fault on the last player that hit it.

But if the ball hits a permanent object after bouncing on the opposing side's court, the opposing side incurs a fault.

Pickled. To lose a game without scoring a single point.

Pickler is a pickleball player who's obsessed with the game since it provides excitement, exercise, mastering new skills, and other reasons, one of which is that it's just plain fun to play.

Poach. In doubles play, it's crossing over to the other side of the court when one partner takes a shot that would normally be the other partner's responsibility. It's usually done to execute a banger put-away shot but can be used strategically. A put-away shot means the opponent cannot react fast enough to successfully hit a return.

Quinned or quinning refers to when you win repeated games and are doing very well. The word combines the name Quinn and the verb winning or Quinning.

Rack. Slang term for a pickleball racket.

Ready position. The ready position is a stance you take before playing starts or your opponent hits the ball. Generally, a ready position means you face in the direction of the ball with both feet on the ground, up on the balls of your feet, a bit more than shoulder-width apart, and holding your paddle out about chest height.

Scorpion. Scorpion refers to an overhead shot done while the person hitting it is in a squatting position. It's sometimes used as an offensive shot instead of a defensive backhand shot.

Tweener. A player returns a shot by hitting the ball between their own legs. Usually done after running after a lob or when a player faces the net and the ball passes between their legs and the only option is to return it by hitting the ball between their own legs.

USAP. The USAP is the governing body of pickleball in the United States. It was formerly the USA Pickleball Association (USAPA) or the US Amateur Pickleball Association (U.S.A.P.A.).

We hope you enjoyed the book!

If you liked the book, we would sincerely appreciate your taking a few moments to leave a brief review.

Thank you again very much!

Bruce Miller and Team Golfwell

About the authors.

Bruce Miller. Lawyer, businessman, world traveler, pickleball player and enthusiast, private pilot, and award-winning author of over 50 books, a few being bestsellers, spends his days writing, studying, and constantly learning of the astounding, unexpected, and amazing events happening in the world today while exploring the brighter side of life.

Bruce wrote the Psychic Mystery/Thriller "Beware the Ides of March: A Novel Based on Psychic Readings" which was awarded the 2023 NYC Big Book Distinguished Favorite.

He's a member of the Australian Golf Media Association, the New Zealand Society of Authors, and the Independent Book Publishers Association.

He also founded the popular Facebook group, "Golf Jokes and Stories" with over 350,000+ followers, and invites you to join!

Team Golfwell are bestselling authors. Their books have sold thousands of copies including several #1 bestsellers in Golf Coaching, Sports humor, and other categories.

We Want to Hear from You!

"There usually is a way to do things better and there is opportunity when you find it." - *Thomas Edison*

We love to hear your thoughts and suggestions on anything and please feel free to contact us at bruce@teamgolfwell.com

Other Books by Bruce Miller [37] and Team Golfwell [38]

"For People Who Have Everything Series (22 Books)" [39]

For the Greatest Cook Who Has It All!

For the Golfer Who Has Everything: A Funny Golf Book

For a Great Fisherman Who Has Everything: A Funny Book for Fishermen

For a Tennis Player Who Has Everything: A Funny Tennis Book

The Funniest Quotations to Brighten Every Day: Brilliant, Inspiring, and Hilarious Thoughts from Great Minds

Jokes for Very Funny Kids (Ages 3 to 7): Funny Jokes, Riddles and More

Jokes for Very Funny Kids (Big & Little): Funny Jokes and Riddles Ages 9 - 12 and up and many more.

And many more…

Index

For a Pickleball Player Who Has It All!

References

[1] "Pickleball popularity exploded last year, with more than 36 million playing the sport", CNBC, https://www.cnbc.com/2023/01/05/pickleball-popularity-explodes-with-more-than-36-million-playing.html
[2] Zane's Guide to 2022 Pickleball Spin Serves - YouTube, YouTube, https://www.youtube.com/watch?v=W-E0-hG7kSI
[3] "Play pickleball at Wollman Rink from April to October!" Central Park.com, https://www.centralpark.com/events/pickleball-at-wollman-rink
[4] Various Leisure-Time Physical Activities Associated With Widely Divergent Life Expectancies: The Copenhagen City Heart Study, Mayo Clinic, https://www.mayoclinicproceedings.org/article/S0025-6196(18)30538-X/fulltext
[5] Ibid.
[6] Ibid.
[7] Guinness World Records, Longest Pickleball rally, https://www.guinnessworldrecords.com/world-records/669898-longest-pickleball-rally
[8] Ibid.
[9] Erne Perry shows us how to do the Erne! YouTube, https://www.youtube.com/watch?v=avFi1rZPb84
[10] Pickleball, Wikipedia, https://en.wikipedia.org/wiki/Pickleball
[11] Ibid.
[12] Pickleball Union, "Playing Pickleball At Over 600 Feet In The Sky!", https://pickleballunion.com/pickleball-in-the-sky/
[13] Ibid.
[14] Simone Jardim, Block volley drills - soft hands, https://www.youtube.com/watch?v=KeA4ffpFWh8

15 IJREP.org, "The Acute and Chronic Physiological Responses to Pickleball in Middle-Aged and Older Adults", https://ijrep.org/the-acute-and-chronic-physiological-responses-to-pickleball-in-middle-aged-and-older-adults/
16 Ibid.
17 Ibid.
18 Everything You Need To Know About Spin in Pickleball (Topspin, Backspin, and Sidespin), Selkirk TV, https://www.youtube.com/watch?v=w1mBDPM_dd4
19 The 4 P's of Pickleball to Stay Injury Free, Post Bulletin, https://www.postbulletin.com/health/practice-the-4-ps-of-pickleball-to-stay-injury-free-with-tips-from-a-mayo-clinic-expert
20 Ibid.
21 Zane's Favorite Third Shot in Pickleball - The Hybrid Drop/Drive, YouTube, https://www.youtube.com/watch?v=68hO0fT73cg
22 Strategies, Doubles Strategies, USA Pickleball, https://usapickleball.org/what-is-pickleball/strategies/doubles-strategies
23 Pickleball: "What Are the Health Benefits of Pickleball?" WebMD.com, https://www.webmd.com/fitness-exercise/what-to-know-about-pickleball
24 Ibid.
25 Ibid.
26 Pickleball and mental health in adults: A systematic review, National Center for Biotechnology Information, https://www.ncbi.nlm.nih.gov/pmc/articles/PMC9988900/
27 Ibid.
28 "The Future of Pickleball: An Economic Perspective", Harvard Economics Review, https://www.economicsreview.org/post/the-future-of-pickleball-an-economic-perspective#
29 Ibid.

30 Pickleball, Wikipedia,
https://en.wikipedia.org/wiki/Pickleball#International_status
31 "Pickleball popularity exploded last year, with more than 36 million playing the sport, CNBC,
https://www.cnbc.com/2023/01/05/pickleball-popularity-explodes-with-more-than-36-million-playing.html#"
32 USA Pickleball Rulebook, p. 46.
33 International Federation of Pickleball, Wikipedia,
https://en.wikipedia.org/wiki/International_Federation_of_Pickleball
34 An unbelievable Joey shot, YouTube,
https://www.youtube.com/watch?v=ehlSuoNWmfU
35 Glossary of pickleball terms, Wikipedia,
https://en.wikipedia.org/wiki/Glossary_of_pickleball_terms
36 The Nasty Nelson shot, Pickleball Minute,
https://www.youtube.com/watch?v=aFH2rfoa2LM
37 https://www.teamgolfwell.com/
38 Ibid.
39 Ibid.

Made in the USA
Monee, IL
21 May 2025